Chamber Music
by H. Voxman

for
THREE CLARINETS, Vol. I

CONTENTS...

Rounds and Catches . . .

RUBANK®

HAL•LEONARD™
CORPORATION
7777 W. BLUEMOUND RD. P.O. BOX 13819 MILWAUKEE, WI 53213

The Three Kings

Bb Clarinets

NICOLAUS

March

from Partita in F

Bb Clarinets

FABER

Minuet I

from Partita in F

Bb Clarinets

FABER

Minuet II

from Partita in F

B♭ Clarinets

FABER

Sarabande

Bb Clarinets

SCHLESWIG

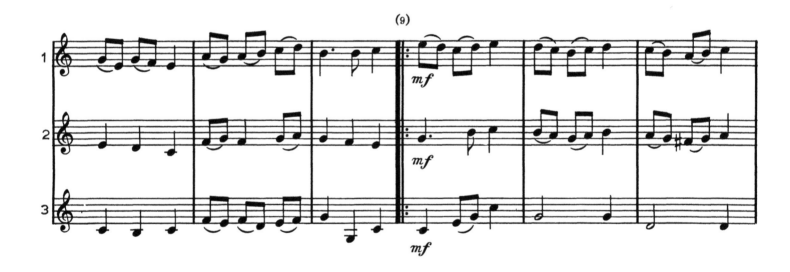

Two Early American Airs

I- CHESTER

Bb Clarinets

Wm. BILLINGS
Arr. by R. Hervig

II- SWEET BETSY FROM PIKE

Bb Clarinets

Early American
Arr. by R. Hervig

Come, Follow Me
(Round)

HILTON

Come, Companions
(Round)

Anon.

Three Old Dutch Dances

I- MAY DANCE

Bb Clarinets

Netherlands

II- ALLEMANDE

Netherlands

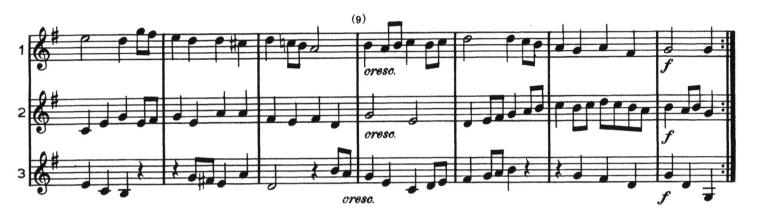

III- GAILLARDE

Netherlands

Entr'acte

from Rosamunde

B♭ Clarinets

SCHUBERT

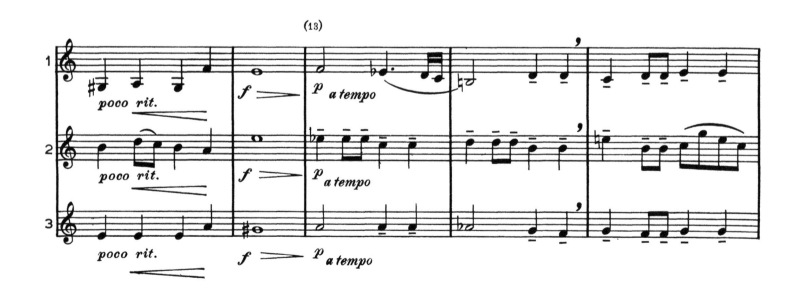

Haste Thee, Nymph
(Round)

ARNOLD

Allegro

B♭ Clarinets

MOZART

Farewell to the Forest

Bb Clarinets

MENDELSSOHN

Drink to Me Only With Thine Eyes

Bb Clarinets

Old English

Begone, Dull Care!

Bb Clarinets

Old English

The Scale
(Round)

BEETHOVEN

Song of the Watchman

Bb Clarinets

GRIEG

The Glass Was Just Tim'd
(Catch)

PURCELL

March

B♭ Clarinets

FISCHER

Old French Song

Bb Clarinets

TSCHAIKOWSKY
Op.39,No.16

Warily!

RAMANN

Soldiers' March

B♭ Clarinets

R. SCHUMANN
Op. 68, No. 2

Old German Dance

Bb Clarinets

Traditional

Great Apollo and Bacchus
(Catch)

PURCELL

23

Sailors' Dance

Bb Clarinets

Netherlands

Gavotte

B♭ Clarinets

MARTINI

Menuet
from Divertimento II

Bb Clarinets

MOZART

Bb Clarinets

Ecossaise

Bb Clarinets

HUMMEL

Menuet

from Trio No.3, Op.57

B♭ Clarinets

BOUFFIL

TRIO

Bourrée
from Royal Fireworks Music

Bb Clarinets

HANDEL

March in C

B♭ Clarinets

KRANZ

Valse Lente

B♭ Clarinets

KRANZ

Menuet

Bb Clarinets

BUTTSTEDT